MUSIC PRACTICE

THE MUSICIAN'S GUIDE TO PRACTICING AND MASTERING YOUR INSTRUMENT LIKE A PROFESSIONAL

BY DAVID DUMAIS

Music Practice: The Musician's Guide to Practicing and Mastering your Instrument like a Professional

Copyright © 2015, by David Dumais

Disclaimer

To my beautiful wife who continuously supports me in all my endeavors.

I love you!

TABLE OF CONTENTS

INTRODUCTION

I want to thank you and congratulate you for buying the book *Music Practice: The Musicians Guide to Practicing and Mastering Your Instrument like a Professional*! I am confident that this book will help you in the practice room and will have a great impact on your journey to whatever career or goals you have chosen for yourself.

While working on my undergraduate degree in clarinet performance, I found myself struggling so much to improve and move ahead in my playing. I felt like I was stuck and hit an unmoveable wall. Some days I would practice five to eight hours a day and not notice any major difference in my playing. Sometimes I found that I improved more when I didn't play! This is when I began my search for the keys to success. This is when I began my continuous search for the best ways to practice.

I began attending masterclasses from internationally renowned professionals on different instruments. I read numerous books, watched multiple videos, and bought programs to help me improve my playing. This book is a compilation of the best practice tips and strategies from the best musicians in the world, musicians including pianists, violinists, trumpeters, and clarinettists. I know that these tips will help you wherever you are in your career.

Thanks again for buying this book - enjoy!

CHAPTER 1: GOAL-SETTING FOR EFFECTIVE PRACTICING

"Setting goals is the first step in turning the invisible into the visible."

-Tony Robbins

Setting goals may be the most crucial step you take in practicing effectively. Of all the tips and advice given in this book, if you had to retain but one idea, this would be the one. Before beginning any practicing or even touching your instrument, make sure you *set goals and write them down*. I cannot emphasize enough its importance. Do not skip this step! Goals not only help you stay organized - they give you direction. Without goals, you cannot even know where you are going, let alone know your destination. Like a ship tossing back and forth against the waves, it is not going anywhere. I'll say it again to make sure this really sticks in your mind: DO NOT SKIP THIS STEP! WRITE DOWN YOUR GOALS!

WRITING YOUR GOALS

Here are a few pointers to make the most use of goal-setting. Ask yourself these questions:

What is my dream job?

If I could have anything I want, what would it be?

If there is only one skill that I could master today, what skill would make the biggest difference in my playing?

These can be your starting points to setting music goals. Once you have your goal in mind, take out a notebook and write it down. Set aside this notebook exclusively for your goals. Make sure you notate your goals in the notebook every day. Do it first thing in the morning or first thing before practicing. To make sure you don't forget, set your notebook on your music stand, on top of your music, or on your instrument. You can also set a reminder on your phone. Do whatever it takes to get it done. Rewriting your goals daily will

inscribe them into your subconscious mind and will continuously giv
focus and direction. Do not concern yourself with how you will achieve
goals. That will come later. Simply be creative, dream big and write d
your goals!

3 KEYS TO WRITING A SUCCESSFUL GOAL

There are three keys to writing an effective goal: the goal must be personal,
positive, and in the present tense. Always begin your goals with the pronoun
"I". Never use negatives such as "not" or "won't". Always write your goal as if
you have already achieved it. Keep all your goals short and to the point.
Finally, set a deadline date for each of your goals.

EXAMPLES OF GOOD GOAL WRITING

I play my C+ scale in sixteenth notes at quarter equals 120 by January 1st,
2016.

I play the Mozart Concerto with complete focus and concentration by
September 30th, 2016.

I am principal oboe of the Philadelphia Orchestra by September 1st, 2016

EXAMPLES OF BAD GOAL WRITING

I **will** play my C+ scale in sixteenth notes at quarter equals 120 by January
1st, 2016. (Future tense)

I **won't make any mistakes** in my Mozart Concerto by September 30th,
2016. (Negative)

I **will** be principal oboe of the Philadelphia Orchestra. (Future tense, No
deadline)

DEADLINES

"When it is obvious that the goals cannot be reached, don't adjust the goals,
adjust the action steps."

-Confucius

Do not worry about missing a deadline. The deadline is there to keep you on track and to keep you focused. Do your best to achieve your goal within your set deadline, but do not beat yourself up if you miss it. Simply set yourself another one and push through. Reflect on why you missed your deadline and make the changes necessary to make sure you don't do it again.

CLARITY

One of the keys to achieving your goals is to be absolutely clear about what it is that you want. Make sure you can picture it in your mind. Make sure you can explain it to somebody. Make sure you can draw it out if possible. Make sure you can see, smell, taste, hear, and feel exactly what it would be like if you had it right now. Every day when you write down your goals, recall these feelings. Remember that we become what we think about most often.

IMPORTANCE OF THOUGHTS

If I tell myself to play through Mozart without making any mistakes, what does my brain think about? Making mistakes. And then what happens? I make mistakes. If I tell you not to think about pink elephants, what do you think about? Pink elephants. It's inevitable. That is how our brains are wired - only thinking of one thing at a time. It will only think about what you tell it to think about, whether positive or negative. Guard your thoughts and keep them focused on what you desire.

PATH TO YOUR GOALS

Once you have all your goals written out (I suggest writing at least 10 goals for the current year), you can set up a plan to achieve your goal. Where do you start? Find someone who has already achieved the goal you set for yourself and do exactly what they did to get to achieve that goal. Save yourself time and don't reinvent the wheel. Model yourself after this individual or group and learn everything you can from them. Commit yourself to continuous improvement and continuous learning every day. Notice how they think and act. Be aware of how they practice, of what they focus on. Figure out their daily routine.

SHIFTING MINDSETS

One of the great turning points in my music career is when I made a shift in thinking about mistakes and failures. I used to always berate myself when I made mistakes in performance or if I messed up a passage in my lesson. I thought that when I made mistakes I was a failure. I was no good.

However, I have since learned that each so-called "failure" is a learning experience. It is a step closer to achieving your goal and to achieving success. Each "failure" builds you up. Each "failure" teaches you and makes you more knowledgeable. My old way of thinking only led me into a downward spiral of frustration and pessimism until I shifted into a positive way of thinking: there is only real failure when you decide to give up and quit. With this kind of mindset, you can only continuously improve, grow, and win.

If you struggle with the same kind of mindset as I did, decide to change your way of thinking. Write down what you will change. Remind yourself of your decision every time you make a mistake or when your old way of thinking tries to sneak in. If you decide to change that today, I can guarantee it will bring you a huge step closer towards accomplishing your goals.

AFFIRMATIONS

After your goals have been written in the morning, the next list you want to write down every day is a list of affirmations to yourself. This may seem strange at first but remember what we know: you become what you think about most often. Write down a list of at least five affirmations of what you are or want to become. Start each affirmation with "I am" when possible. Write these affirmations every day right after writing down your goals. Your list may look something like this:

I am able

I am strong

I am decisive

I am persistent

I am committed

TO–Do List

The next list you need to write is your daily to-do list. Write down all the things you need to do today. This can be in point form. Once you've done this, prioritize your list. Write a number one on your top priority, then two and so on. This is crucial! It will keep you organized and focused on your most important tasks. This will set you apart from most other people who don't prioritize their to-do list. Make sure to always follow your list and always complete the first task before moving on to the next.

Once again, this is the most important chapter in this book. It may seem trite but it makes the biggest difference in the long run. Goal-setting is the starting point to your success.

CHAPTER 2: HAVING AN ENGAGING PRACTICE SESSION

"Mastering music is more than learning technical skills. Practicing is about quality, not quantity. Some days I practice for hours; other days it will be just a few minutes."

-Yo-Yo Ma

Having an engaging practice session is important. This is what will keep you motivated to practice your instrument while really enjoying your practice. In order to do this, you must keep your mind engaged so that it never wanders off. It must be completely focused on the task at hand. The most efficient method of doing this is by varying your practice and varying it often. In this chapter, I want to show five tips to vary your practice and to stay fully engaged for the whole duration of you practice sessions.

DIVIDE YOUR REPERTOIRE

Vary your practice by dividing up your repertoire in two. Half will be for day one and the other for day two. Try to split it as evenly as possible in terms of categories. For example, each day have: one solo, one study, some technique, and a few excerpts. Make sure that you never practice the same music two days in a row. Doing this will help you stay organized, and will make it really easy for you to play through all of your music without ever having to skip a piece due to lack of time. This tip helps with always having something new to work on. Note that as you approach a performance, about a month in advance, switch to playing your performance repertoire every day.

TIME

A key to effectively engaging your brain is in knowing how much time to spend on a piece, movement, or excerpt. You should only be spending about 5-10 minutes MAX on any given piece. The only exception would be when you are practicing a run-through or practicing a performance from beginning to the end. For example, if you are having trouble with the first five notes of a C+ scale, you should be spending a maximum of 5-10 minutes working on those five notes and then move on to a different scale. If you are having trouble with the opening of a piece, spend 5-10 minutes on it and then move on to a different piece.

I have heard it said that the less time you spend on an excerpt at one time, the better. I know some will only spend two minutes max and then move on to another excerpt. For myself, I have found 5-10 minutes to be a stable amount of time.

VARIATIONS WITHIN THE 5-10 MINUTES

Vary your practice even more within your 5-10 minute timeslot. Switch between different rhythmic patterns, tempos, and articulations every 2-3 minutes. If you're working on a particular 16th note run, for example, you can play dotted rhythms for 2-3 minutes then switch to straight 16th notes for 2-3 minutes, and then play inverted dotted rhythms for 2-3 minutes. You can also go back and forth between different sections of an excerpt every 2-3 minutes.

Here is one example for how to set up an engaging 5-10 minutes of practice:

Section A - Rhythm 1 - 2 minutes

Section B - Rhythm 2 - 2 minutes

Section A - Rhythm 2 - 2 minutes

Section B - Rhythm 1 - 2 minutes

INSTRUMENT TO NON-INSTRUMENT

Switching every 10 minutes between your instrument and ear training/ sight-singing is another way to vary your practice. You could do 10 minutes of instrument practice, 10 minutes of sight-singing practice, 10 minutes of instrument practice, and then 10 minutes of ear training.

BREAKS

Taking many breaks is an effective way to stay engaged and vary your practice. It may seem contradictory at first. How are you staying engaged when you are not practicing at all? This is because our brains tend to remember best the beginning of an activity and the ending of an activity; like how the brain remembers best the opening and closing of a movie, and the introduction and conclusion of a speech. Therefore, the more beginnings and endings you create, the better you will learn, recall, and remember your music. A good amount of time for a break is 15 minutes for every 45 minutes or so of practicing. Be sure that you do something completely separate from music on your break. Go wash the dishes, read, or do a bit of homework. Whatever you decide to do during your break shouldn't be music related.

Engaging practice forces you to make the most of your practice time. Perhaps that is why it is so effective; there is no room for wasted time. Ask the **golden question** to make sure you are always practicing what you need to practice: What one section of this piece that if I mastered today would make the biggest difference in my playing? Spend no more than 10 minutes per section. Vary often and switch frequently so that your brain always has something new to focus on and think about. When you get to the point where you can do this regularly, you will have consistently effective and engaging practices sessions.

Always remember: variation is the key to engaging practice.

CHAPTER 3: 24 TRICKS FOR METRONOME PRACTICE WITH AND WITHOUT YOUR INSTRUMENT

"The objection, sometimes heard, that using a metronome tends to make a player mechanical, is not founded on facts. Indeed, the students who play the most artistically are those who have been the most faithful in the use of their metronome when learning their pieces."

-Josephine Menuez

The best proven method to perfecting rhythm and pulse is to practice with the metronome. You must do this consistently every day! I know many people do not like practicing with the metronome, but this is the key to rhythmic success. In this first section, I will be presenting you 15 ways to practice with the metronome while improving your skill.

METRONOME PRACTICE WITH YOUR INSTRUMENT

The basic method of practicing with the metronome is to just have it ticking on each beat and playing the music at that pace. This is fine to start with but to move forward in becoming an advanced player, it will do you no good to stick with only this kind of practicing.

Here are a few tips to vary your practice and improve your rhythm and inner pulse. For the purpose of these examples, let us assume we are in 4/4 time and playing a passage in sixteenth notes:

1. Set subdivisions on the metronome to the smallest note value that is in the passage you are working on. In this case, the smallest note value is a sixteenth note. Subdivide each beat into sixteenth notes on your metronome and play through the passage with this subdivision. Make sure all notes are played accurately.

2. Alternate starting on different parts of the subdivided basic beat. In this case, set subdivisions on the metronome to sixteenth notes and play through

the passage starting on the first 16th click of the metronome (i.e. on the beginning of the quarter note- the basic beat). After practicing that, shift to starting on the second 16th subdivided click of the metronome. For the next round, shift to the third 16th, and the next time on the fourth 16th subdivided click of the metronome.

3. You can also practice starting at different points of the passage. First, start the passage at the beginning, on the first note, like normal. Then, play from the middle of the passage, from let's say the 13rd note. Then, play from the 7th note of the passage. Keep varying it by starting on different notes.

4. Once you become comfortable with the shortest note value subdivisions, you can double the metronome subdivision within the beat. In this case, a sixteenth subdivision would then become an eighth. Set the metronome to have every beat subdivide in eighth notes and practice the passage with this subdivision.

5. If your metronome allows it, turn off the emphasis on the basic beats but keep the subdivisions so that there is only one pitch of tone for all clicks. This way, you force yourself to feel all the beats. If your metronome does not allow you to do this, you can create a similar pattern using a different method: for example, if the tempo of the passage is 60 beats per minute (bpm) in sixteenth notes, you would set your metronome without subdivisions to 240 bpm (60x4). This is the same as 16th note subdivisions at 60 bpm but without the emphasis click on every quarter note. Now play through the passage with the non-emphasised metronome pattern.

6. If possible, walk around in tempo while playing the passage or piece of music. This will help you stay relaxed and synchronize your body with your playing.

7. Articulate subdivisions of longer held notes. The reason for this is because players tend to cut short and rush the value of the longer notes. Articulating subdivisions of any note one beat in length and longer will help keep the note values precise.

8. If you do not require your mouth to play your instrument, count out loud when you are playing. Use subdivisions when counting. In this case, you

would be counting: 1 e & a, 2 e & a, 3 e & a, 4 e & a. If you do play a wind instrument, you could finger the passage while counting out loud.

9. Practice playing duplets/quadruplets against triplet subdivisions on the metronome. For triplet passages, practice playing against duplet/quadruplet subdivisions on the metronome. In this case, set your metronome to triplet subdivisions while playing your 16th note passage. This will add a new challenge to your practice.

10. The most effective way I have learned to internalize rhythm and pulse is to halve the length of the beats per minute on the metronome. For example, if the piece of music is played at 60 bmp, then I will set the metronome to 30 bmp. This way I have to play two beats of music within one click of the metronome. This forces you to feel and know exactly where the two beats sit.

Once you are very comfortable with the tips mentioned above, try challenging yourself further by playing with one click per measure. This will help you develop your inner pulse. For example, playing in a 4/4 time signature:

1. Play the passage so that the metronome click is on the downbeat (beat 1).

2. Play the passage so that the metronome click is on the 2nd beat (beat 2).

3. Play the passage so that the metronome click is half-way through the measure (beat 3).

4. Play the passage so that the metronome click is on the upbeat of the measure (beat 4).

I know and I have heard many teachers say that you should practice as much with the metronome as without it. In my experience, the closer I got to being confident playing 1 measure in 1 click, the better I played without the metronome. I would strongly recommend playing a lot with the metronome at 1 click per measure and challenging yourself beyond that. Play 1 click for every 2 measures, even for 3 or 4 measures depending on the speed of the piece. This is what will help you play in time without a metronome.

Do not rush into all of these practice techniques at once. It could take a few weeks to be completely comfortable with just one of these steps. Pick one of the above tips and stick with it every day until it is absorbed in your system and becomes habit. Repeat picking and mastering a new tip until all of those practice approaches become effortless to use at a moment's notice.

I like to encourage students to be creative and come up with their own ways of practicing with the metronome that helps them. If some of these tips can spark your imagination into new ways of practicing, then try it and expand your skills.

So far, I have shown different ways and variations on how to practice rhythm and pulse with the metronome and with your instrument. In this next section, I want to show some rewarding and challenging techniques to practice rhythm and internalizing pulse without your instrument. It may not be the most amusing, but it can make a big difference in your playing.

METRONOME PRACTICE WITHOUT YOUR INSTRUMENT

"The biggest difference between a professional musician and an amateur is pulse and rhythm."

-Anonymous

In this section, I want to show you ten different ways to nail down rhythms without using your instrument. This will not only be useful when playing by yourself but also in an ensemble setting, be it in a band, orchestra, or with piano accompaniment. Practicing these different techniques for even as little as 5-10 minutes a day will dramatically improve your sense of time and will give you confidence to play in any given situation, no matter the complexity of the rhythms.

The simple way to begin is to choose a piece of music with which you are rhythmically struggling, turn on your metronome, and clap only one rhythm (ex: the melody only). You can also sing the rhythms with a simple "da" syllable instead of clapping. You can use solfège syllables to test your mastery of that rhythm when the "da" syllable becomes too easy. Or, stay on the same pitch to focus on practicing rhythms. If your instrument has other voices, go through each one that needs work, one at a time. Work on trouble spots before moving on.

The following are steps to increase your inner pulse. Follow these steps in order and do not skip any as they grow in level of difficulty. Keep the metronome on throughout each of these exercises. For these exercises, let's assume we are working on the melody:

1. Count the beats OUT LOUD and clap the melody in your hands.

2. Clap the beats with your hands and sing the melody (using the "da" syllable).

3. Walk (don't run) around the room and clap the melody. Take only one step for each beat or, if that is too fast, take one step for every two beats or for each measure.

4. Walk (don't run) around the room and sing the melody. Again, make sure each step is in time.

5. Conduct the meter pattern while singing the melody.

6. Conduct the meter pattern while walking and singing the melody.

The following steps are for multiple voices. If you are a single-voice instrument, choose the melody of your instrument and the melody of the piano accompaniment.

7. Tap your hands on your thighs. The right hand taps the basic beat and the left hand taps the piano voice. If the piano has multiple voices, choose any one of the piano voices - usually the melody is best. Sing the melody of your instrument.

8. Tap your hands on your thighs. The right hand is the rhythm of the melody and the left hand is the rhythm of the piano.

9. Tap your hands on your thighs. The right hand is the rhythm of the melody and the left hand is the rhythm of the piano. Count OUT LOUD.

10. Tap your hands on your thighs. The right hand is the piano soprano voice and the left hand is the piano bass voice. Sing your instrumental part.

Once you get comfortable with these, you can combine the exercises further to make them more challenging. Have fun and create your own exercises.

CHAPTER 4: 5 METHODS TO PRACTICE INTONATION

"Of course the most difficult thing on the violin is always intonation. The second one is rhythm. If you play in tune, in time with a good sound that's already high level. Those three are the main things."

-Ruggiero Ricci

Intonation is a huge factor that separates amateur musicians from professional musicians. As I have heard many teachers say, "If you are not in tune, you are playing the wrong note." Harsh as it may sound, this is the reality; intonation is that important.

EAR TRAINING

Intonation is first and foremost an ear challenge. If you can't hear that a note is out of tune, you can't hear it in tune. Additionally, just because you can hear it out of tune, it doesn't mean you can hear it in tune. What can you do to fix this? Ear training!

Ear training may not always be the most amusing, but 10-15 minutes a day can have a substantial impact in the long run. Here are a few items you will want to practice:

Interval Identification

Chord Identification

Chord Inversions

Melodic Dictation

Pitch Training

Make sure to work on these slowly and incrementally. Train yourself one interval at a time if you need to. Don't go to the hardest intervals unless you are ready to work at that level.

There are many apps you can download for free on your phone to practice these, such as:

Perfect Ear 2: http://bit.ly/1JGeGtf

My Ear Trainer: http://bit.ly/1IzXjMh

Functional Ear Trainer: http://bit.ly/1F62ykj

Complete Ear Trainer: http://bit.ly/1PKE82z

You can also check out these websites for further practice:

http://www.absolutepitchlessons.com/

https://www.teoria.com/en/exercises/

http://www.earbeater.com/

http://bit.ly/1Egk55V

DRONE PRACTICE

Drone practice can be very effective for training your ear. When practicing, turn on the drone on your tuner or metronome and play through the piece. You will be able to notice immediately which notes are out of tune. Use this method also when practicing scales and arpeggios.

Make the drone note the tonic of the piece. You can also select the dominant for variation. Another choice can be the highest note of the piece or the lowest note of the piece as these notes tend to be out of tune. Also, you can choose a note with which you know you are having trouble tuning.

A key to drone practice is not to practice fixing the intonation, but rather to practice playing in tune. What do I mean? Do not practice playing the note and then slowly working your pitch down/up to the correct tuning. Rather, practice hitting the right note with the correct intonation right away, and at tempo. If you cannot pitch the note immediately, come back to it every day and keep practicing it.

Singing

Along with ear training, singing may be the most effective way to train your ear and improve your intonation. Through singing, you learn to hear the pitch in your mind before producing the sound, which is an essential skill when playing your instrument.

Practice singing scales and arpeggios. Practice singing your pieces. You can sing with the drone on for an additional challenge.

Practicing sight-singing will improve your ear's ability to differentiate the relationship between intervals. It will train your ear to hear notes in relation to the tonic. When sight-singing, play a tonic triad on a keyboard to get the tonic in your mind's ear. Sing the whole piece or passage in tempo without any other reference to the keyboard. Go back and work on trouble sections.

Recordings

One of the ways that I began to make a big an improvement in my intonation was when I started playing with recordings. This is a great way to match your sound and improve tuning. Choose a quality recording from a professional musician. Also, sing your part along with the recording. If you are lucky, you may find a recording of just the accompaniment.

Transpose

Transposing your music into different keys can be challenging and may also seem like a waste of time because you have to relearn all the notes, but it can work wonders. Practicing transposing your music into different keys will help you hear the relationship between notes so that no matter the key or your instrument's tendencies, you know the distance between the intervals. You will be able to play the correct intervals in any key, in addition to improving transposing skills.

The purpose of these methods is so that eventually you can hear pitches in your mind, hear them in tune in relation to each other, and be able to physically reproduce them. The mind's ear will automatically help the body play the instrument in tune once the ear has done adequate training.

CHAPTER 5: SLOW PRACTICE VS. FAST PRACTICE

"If there is no struggle, there is no progress."

-Frederick Douglass

There is much talk about how musicians should practice, but it is commonly agreed that slow practice is definitely necessary for advancement and mastery of your craft. Little talk is usually given about fast practice. Does fast practice exist? I never heard any of my teachers talk about fast practice until after I graduated with my bachelor's degree. In this chapter I want to show you seven different ways of practicing slowly but also up to tempo. As well, I will explain not only the advantages and disadvantages of slow and fast practice but also the necessity of both.

SLOW PRACTICE

This kind of practice may seem boring, but it can actually feel quite fulfilling if you do it properly. A great way to think of slow practice is to think of it as slow motion practice. It should sound the same as if it were played full speed, but in slow motion. You need to play with the same dynamics, expressions, and phrase direction.

It is important that you keep the direction of the music when practicing slowly. Try phrase-mapping: this is when you plan out each phrase in the music, marking in your score where the phrase begins, where the climax or peak is, and where it ends. Do this for every phrase in your piece and play it the way you marked it.

Here are three approaches to practicing slowly:

Slow with incremental increases approach: Begin with the metronome marking at half the desired performance speed (if that is still too fast, go slower). Play until it becomes easier. Now, as the name of this approach suggests, simply increase the metronome marking in incremental amounts. Repeat until you reach the desired tempo.

Half speed-full speed approach: For this approach, alternate between half tempo and full performance tempo.

Two-steps forward, one-step back approach: Begin by putting the metronome at half tempo of the desired performance speed (if that is still too fast, go slower). Practice the passage at this speed until it becomes a bit easier. Then, increase the metronome marking a considerable amount to a tempo at which you struggle with the music. Repeat the passage a few times until it becomes easier to play and then bring the metronome down to a few markings to just above the half tempo (where you first started). Play the passage again; the music should feel easier to play. Repeat this process until you arrive at the desired performance speed.

ADVANTAGES AND DISADVANTAGES OF SLOW PRACTICE

The best time to use slow practice is when you are learning new pieces. This will help you to learn the notes, phrases, and expressions very quickly. It is also great to help you identify challenging sections right down to the challenging note or interval. Practicing slowly can give you a heightened sense of awareness of your own body and of your playing. This is useful for any finger movement or embouchure challenges that may arise.

The disadvantage of practicing slowly is that your body doesn't move and play the same during slow practice as it does during fast practice. Your brain doesn't think the same when you play slowly as when you play fast. If you do too much slow practice, it can actually be detrimental to your performance. As soon as you move up to performance speed, your brain will only be trying to catch up to the music. This inevitably leads to mistakes. However, all of this can be avoided using fast practice to complement slow practice.

FAST PRACTICE

There are many ways to practice your music at performance speed, but I will show you a few proven ways that work very effectively. These can also be applied to slow practice. As with slow practice, ensure you play the same dynamics, expressions, and phrase direction as written for fast practice. Here are 4 approaches:

Hold-a-note approach: For this approach, play the passage at performance speed and when you arrive at a note that is challenging, hold it for four beats or more (as if it were a long tone). This stabilizes the pitch and tone with which you have difficulty executing. If applicable, finish the rest of the phrase afterwards. Make sure you play past the note and through the passage to keep the direction and phrase of the music. Repeat this multiple times. Hold different notes if necessary.

Looping approach: This approach is one of the most effective and challenging ways to do fast practice. For this approach, start by looping (repeating) a small group of notes in tempo, over and over again for as long as you can. Be absolutely sure that you are 100% precise with the tempo. This approach must be performed with the metronome. Challenge yourself to see how many times you can loop a group of notes, phrase, or section.

Shortened long tone approach: This approach is a combination of Hold-a-note and Looping. Loop a group of notes once and when you land on the note you started on, hold it for four beats. Repeat the loop and the next time you land on the starting note, hold it for three beats. Repeat and keep on shortening the amount of time spent on the held note.

Add-a-note approach: This approach is exactly as the name suggests. Start with only one note. Play this one note in time and repeat it until you are comfortable with it. Then, add a note. Play only these two notes. Repeat them over and over. When you are comfortable and it becomes easier to play, add a note. Repeat. You could learn an entire piece using only this method and never even have to do slow practice!

Note:

Be patient! Fast-practicing is not a quick-fix method, but once you have a section or a piece learned this way, you will be able to transfer those skills to all other pieces. Start by accepting where you are; this is your current skill level. If on the first day all you can play is one or two notes, then so be it. Accept that and come back to it the next day. Don't worry if your fingers are not fast enough, or if your embouchure is not flexible enough. That is the point of these exercises: they improve muscle memory and flexibility. Practice this skill every day and you will move forward and improve quickly.

One more point: fast practice is very effective for practicing slow pieces. Practice slow pieces at double speed. This helps you get a great sense of direction and rhythm for the piece. When you slow it back down you will feel much more confident with the rhythms and phrases.

Advantages and Disadvantages of Fast Practicing

The greatest advantage to fast practicing is that you are training your brain to perform at your performance tempo. Your brain learns to read the music quickly so that when you do get it comfortably up to performance speed, it suddenly doesn't seem too fast anymore. Your brain trains your ear to hear what it sounds like fast. It doesn't have to worry about every single note being in tune because it already knows where that is (especially if you practice this with a drone). This approach to practicing also trains muscle memory and fluid air flow.

The disadvantage to this sort of practicing is that it can take long a very long time to learn a new piece of music. It can also be challenging to practice your piece musically with expression at the same time as learning the piece fast right off the bat.

Conclusion

A combination of both slow and fast practice is necessary: slow practice when you are first learning a new piece of music and fast practice when you have learned the notes and are ready to make it performance worthy. Do not get caught practicing slowly over a long period of time, but rather only enough time to learn and be comfortable with the piece of music.

CHAPTER 6: PRACTICING PERFORMING

"There is nothing better than adversity. Every defeat, every heartbreak, every loss, contains its own seed, its own lesson on how to improve your performance the next time."

-Malcolm X

Performance practice is a topic that can often be neglected; what constitutes great stage presence is also often omitted from lessons. In this chapter I will show two ways to practice performing and some tips and tricks to continually improve upon it.

RUN-THROUGHS

Performance practice is a gradual process. You must begin small and grow bigger and bigger for the greatest results. Here are steps to accomplishing this:

1. Private Run-throughs

Before you start playing a run-through, take some time to relax both your body and your mind. Close your eyes and focus on your breathing for 5-10 inhales/exhales. Just feel the air going in and out of your lungs. Feel the air on your lips and nostrils. Feel your lungs expand. Clear your mind of any thoughts.

Practice performing through your piece or your entire recital from the beginning to the end. Make it stress-free. Use a quiet room with as few distractions as possible. If you make a mistake or have a mind blank, KEEP PLAYING! Stopping will only train your brain to stop at mistakes. We cannot do that in real performances.

After the run-through, ask yourself, "What did I do well and would I do differently next time?" **Do not ask**, "Where did I make mistakes or why did I make a mistake?"

Be aware of where the mistakes were, but do not focus your attention on it. This will only focus your mind and sub-conscious to the mistakes and increase the likeliness of doing them again next time.

Make a good quality recording of yourself so that you can go back and find areas that need improvement.

Put up pictures in front of you of your family members where you normally practice, or perhaps of professional musicians that you admire. You can even put up some of your stuffed toys in front of you. I sometimes like to put pictures of a large crowd or a view from a stage on my computer and glance at it while performing.

Next, you can add very soft white noise or a distraction such a quiet radio playing in the background. Start off soft until you get comfortable with the distraction, then you can incrementally raise the volume. Do not rush this process.

2. Performance Group

Create for yourself a performance group. This is a group of close friends that can perform for each other. These friends should be honest and good friends so that they can build you up and give constructive criticism.

Play through your pieces for your performance group. Learn also to listen to your friends play by listening for what they do well and what they can improve on. Increasing your listening skills will improve your own playing.

Find friends that play the same instrument as you, but also different instruments. Groups made up of the same instruments tend to get caught up about instrument-specific challenges. Having diverse players from different instrument groups will enable your group to catch and hear things differently.

3. Public Performance

Once you have gone through the above two steps, you are ready to begin public performances. Start out with a low-stress public performance. This may be playing for your studio, for a teacher, or in a senior's home.

Gradually increase the stress in your performance. If that means playing in front of a large audience, you can start by doing a recital for your family. Then, you can find other friends to put a recital together and invite more people.

TIPS AND TRICKS

Here are a few tips and tricks to keep in mind when practicing performing:

ALWAYS play the way you would in an actual concert. Practice walking into your practice room as if it were the stage. Take a bow and hear the audience clapping.

Make sure you walk confidently with your chest up and your eyes up. (Look down if you need to in order to use the stairs!) Make sure you acknowledge your audience by looking out at them.

Plan what you will do before you start playing: tune your instrument, place your bow on the string, moisten your reed, hear the music in your mind, and place your music on the stand... Whatever it is that you will do before playing that first note, plan it.

At the end of your performance take a bow, even if there is no response from the audience.

MENTAL PRACTICE

Visualization is a practice technique that is rarely taught and yet is proven to be very effective and used by most highly successful people. Use this technique to imagine touching, smelling, hearing, seeing, and tasting. Imagine with material you know very well or it could cause more harm than good. If you do not have the proper skill and muscle memory set in place, you could be learning the wrong feelings or the wrong images associated with visualization. Here are a few points to get you started:

Begin by sitting down comfortably in a quiet area. Close your eyes and breathe in through your nose and out through your mouth. Be completely relaxed, focusing on your inhale and on your exhale. Do this for about 10 inhales and exhales.

Now, with your eyes always closed, begin by picking up your instrument in your mind. How does it feel? How does it look? Be very aware of all your senses.

Envision your regular routine before you begin playing your piece and play through your piece as you normally would if you were practicing with your instrument. Do not stop if you make mistakes. Play your piece mentally from beginning to the end. At the end you will be able to go back and fix sections that need work. If you find it too challenging to mentally rehearse your piece in its entirety, then visualize one section at a time.

Make visualization as similar as possible to your regular practice and performance. Be aware of how your hands and fingers feel. Be aware of how your embouchure feels. Be aware of how your body feels standing in front of an audience. Notice how your mouthpiece tastes in your mouth. Observe what you look like from a first person point of view and from a third person point of view. What does the room smell like and what sounds do you hear? Incorporate each sense one at a time when visualizing.

Visualize performing in different locations: big halls, small churches, or intimate stages. Start with a small crowd and then eventually work your way up to a larger crowd. Hear what they sound like.

Feel the heat of the stage light and see the audience in the dark with all the lights dimmed. Make your imagination as vivid as possible. Try to improve upon your imagination one visualization session at a time.

If you are new to this kind of practice, start by visualizing for two minutes at a time. Slowly increase the duration every time you go back to practicing it. Some professionals will spend up to an hour running through their repertoire.

CHAPTER 7: 10 STRATEGIES TO PRACTICE MEMORIZATION

"Your unconscious memory is virtually perfect. It is your conscious recall that is suspect."

-Brian Tracy

Having a memory slip is probably one of the most embarrassing things that can happen to a musician. Drawing a blank is feared by all and yet none are immune to it. It is something we must work at. However, it is important to know that our problem with memory is not so much memorizing the material. Everybody is an expert at memorizing anything. The problem comes when we try to recall the information we have stored in our brains. This is what we want to work on and improve. Research shows that the best way to do this is through the five senses. If you can store and practice retrieving memory through each of the senses, you will have greater recall. In our role as musicians, we will only focus on the main three senses that we use when playing, which are sight, sound, and touch (physical).

STRATEGY #1: ONE MEASURE AT A TIME

Learn your piece of music one measure at a time. Start at the beginning of your piece and play the first measure once with the score in front of you. Turn away and play it now four times without the score. Once you begin to feel more comfortable with it, add the second measure. Again, play the first two measures once while looking at the score, then four times without the score. Repeat this memorization process and keep on adding measures one at a time. Do this same process beginning in the middle of the piece. Do it starting with the last measure of the piece as well, and work your way backwards. This type of practice will help strengthen your aural memory.

Once you start having multiple bars together, group the measures together into phrases and sub-phrases. When you have a few phrases memorized, group them together to make a "paragraph" of music. When you have a few "paragraphs" memorized, group them more to make "chapters" of music.

The music will be like a story. It may help you to mark each section of your story on the score. This chunking process will help you organize and understand the music at a deeper level, thereby helping you memorize it.

STRATEGY #2: ASSIGN MEANING

Assign meaning to each section of your music as well as to the piece as a whole. Be creative and assign emotions and feelings that the music depicts. Create a story with different characters and assign them specific names. Perhaps the characters are dialoguing. Write out the names of the characters and what they are saying on a separate piece of paper or directly on the score. This will engage your physical, visual, and auditory senses, especially if you speak it out loud. You can associate images and pictures that you feel the music portrays. Print out, make, or draw them yourself. You could even attach them to the score. This will engage your visual and physical senses. Be sure to identify all phrases to help you generate these different ideas. Use your imagination and be creative!

STRATEGY #3: LOCI METHOD

This memory strategy is similar to strategy #2, but the difference is that it links new information with familiar information, routines, or places. Associate the music you want to memorize to people that you know. For example, one phrase may be your father and the next your mother. How do the phrases sound like or characterize them? Describe it out loud and write it down to engage your aural and physical senses. You could also associate rooms in your house to sections of the music. For example, the beginning of the music is your front door and front hall. The next section of music is your living room and the next, your kitchen. As you progress through the piece of music, you make your way through your entire house. It is a journey. Map out your journey and describe it. Mark down how certain sections of the music is like a particular room in your house. Do this for each room. You can also use this idea to go through a park that you may be familiar with. Any journey, road, or event that you are well accustomed to, can be used to be associated with the music.

STRATEGY #4: SING

Singing your music will work your aural sense to memorize your music. This will help you remember the tune and pitches, whether or not it is a melody.

STRATEGY #5: COLOUR

Choose colours for each section of your music. Colour the entire staff of each section or phrase in different colours. You could even try assigning specific notes to specific colours. For example, every "C" would be coloured in blue and every "D" in green. Do this for all the notes, as it helps your visual sense. You may want to photocopy the music if you do not want to write on the original. Visit this website for preassigned colours to music notes: http://musicalcolors.com/tst/development.html

STRATEGY #6: WRITE IT OUT

Rewrite the entire score on a blank sheet of staff paper, doing sections at a time. Make sure to include the tempo markings, dynamics, articulations and any other markings in the music. See how much you can remember by rewriting the music without looking at the score. This strategy will help you to study your score and to know it very well.

STRATEGY #7: ANALYSE THE MUSIC

Go through your music and mark down chord progressions. Additionally, identify the different sections of the piece, such as: the exposition, development, and recapitulation. This will be a helpful way to visually understand the music and a new way to see the musical progression of the piece.

STRATEGY #8: VISUALIZE

Practice playing through your piece in your mind. Sit down in a quiet area with your eyes closed and hear the music from the beginning to the end in your mind's ear. If you draw a blank anywhere, go back and listen to that section again on a recording. Hear the music in your mind until you do not need the recording any more.

Practice also seeing the notes on paper. See all the notes where they are placed. Do this from beginning to the end and go back to where you drew blanks. Repeat as well by practicing in your mind what it would feel like to play the notes on your instrument.

STRATEGY #9: PLAY WITHOUT SOUND

Try playing through a piece, section, or an entire movement on your instrument by fingering the notes without making any sound. See how far you can get. Fix and repeat the spots where you had a memory slip.

For wind instrumentalists, you can blow air patterns that follow the phrases. Add fingering to the air patterns. Be sure to stay relaxed, blow steady air, and breathe where you normally would, paying attention to phrasing and articulation.

STRATEGY #10: REPETITION

Of course, the ultimate way to memorize music is through repetition. Play and repeat your music with your eyes closed and your eyes opened. Go through your music right before you go to bed. The brain rehearses and goes through the lasts things we do right before sleeping. Practice memorization and repetition every day, even if only for a few minutes.

CHAPTER 8: 10 MUST-HAVE PRACTI
HABITS

"The only proper way to eliminate bad habits is to replace them with good ones."

-Jerome Hines

"We first make our habits, and then our habits make us."

-John Dryden

Habits are a very important part of success. It has been said that successful people are simply those with successful habits. If programmed properly, habits can lead to consistent success, and if not, they will lead to consistent failure. Habits are at the core of who we are and what we do. Changing just one habit can change the course of your life.

HABIT #1: GOAL-SETTING

This is the most important habit to form if you are not already doing it. If you have not read Chapter 1, I strongly suggest going back and reading it. If you already have, read it over to get a better understanding of its importance and of how to set goals.

Make sure you commit to writing down all your goals. Set yourself goals for the year, the month, the week, and the day. Be sure to track your success throughout the day, week, and month as you accomplish your goals.

HABIT #2: PLAN YOUR PRACTICE

Be absolutely sure that you plan your practice in two ways. First, write your practice time into your agenda. Mark out specific times throughout the day that will be reserved solely for practicing your instrument. Second, write out specifically what you will be practicing in a practice log. This can be a journal or a simple spiral notebook. For example, mark down which scales you will practice, at what tempo, and for how long. Detail all the music you will practice by planning which piece of music you will play, from which point in the music, at what tempo, for how long, etc. Commit this habit to writing. It may seem counterintuitive to spend time to plan, but planning well eliminates wasted time.

HABIT #3: PRIORITIZE

Be result-oriented by always prioritizing your practice. What needs the greatest amount of practice? What do I need to learn today or this week? My favourite question to ask is the golden question: If I could master any piece I am learning or any skill I am learning, which one would make the biggest difference in my playing right now? Which section? Which interval? Which note? Prioritize and practice!

HABIT #4: REWARD

Practice the habit of rewarding yourself when you accomplish your goals. This can be as simple as saying to yourself "good job!", or cheering, or allowing yourself to have a treat. This may appear silly to those around you, but know that you are building a positive habit that will increase your motivation and self-confidence. Find a way to begin to train your mind to associate goal accomplishments with rewards and good feelings.

HABIT #5: ROUTINE

Set yourself a daily routine and stick to it because humans are creatures of habits. Do your best to be consistent with your practice times every day. Find a time during the day when you practice at your best. For most people, this is early in the morning or late at night. Be sure to take one day completely off every week. Use this day to rest your mind and your body to begin anew for the next week. If you can get into a successful daily routine and follow the habits in this chapter, you will be able to consistently return to them every day. You will grow upon each day of practice and improve faster than you ever have before.

HABIT #6: EASE OF PRACTICE

Be sure that it is absolutely easy for you to start practicing at any time throughout the day. Make your practice room as accessible as possible. Always have your stand set up with your music ready on it. Have a pencil on the stand, a comfortable chair set up, a tuner and metronome ready nearby, and your instrument set up and ready to play. Turn off your phone, computer, or any distractions. Make it as easy as possible for yourself. Do not allow yourself any excuse for not practicing. Have everything you need ready to go so that you can start practicing in less than one minute of you deciding to practice.

HABIT #7: METRONOME AND TUNER

Be sure to always have your metronome and tuner with you and to practice extensively with them. Practicing with a metronome and tuner accelerates your improvement. Be sure to use a metronome that can subdivide at least to sixteenth notes. If you do not have one, you can use the following free online metronomes:

http://metronomer.com/

http://www.onlinetunermetronome.com/

http://bestdrumtrainer.com/tt/

HABIT #8: PATIENCE

The habit of patience is a challenging habit to master, but it must be practiced continually to become a great musician. It doesn't matter who you are: Yo-Yo Ma, Itzhak Pearlman, or Lang Lang; everyone has to practice and be patient. Yes, perhaps some are born with innate abilities, but all must develop their skills, which demands patience. Accept where you are today, be patient, and practice. It is as the saying goes: slowly but surely wins the race.

HABIT #9: SELF-DISCIPLINE

Self-discipline is the ability to get yourself to practice whether you feel like it or not. Those who have the ability to practice even when they do not want to are those who get ahead. Become one of those people. The more you force yourself to practice when you don't feel like it, the easier it becomes until eventually you can command yourself to practice at any time throughout the day despite how you feel. If you struggle with practicing on command, practice for only five minutes to start. Incrementally increase the time whenever you feel like you have to force yourself to practice.

Habit #10: Perform, Don't Practice

Adopt the mindset that every time you pick up your instrument, you are performing. Whether you are alone at home, in a practice room, in front of friends or at a rehearsal, you are performing. Never play on your instrument in a way that you would not play in a concert. DO NOT doodle around on your instrument, EVER! You can improvise if you wish, but do not doodle. Be aware of when you lose focus or make a mistake because what you repeat continuously will eventually become habit. Whether it's a good habit or not, or a habit you want or not, your subconscious mind doesn't care. Whatever you repeat will become a habit. Decide that each time you pick up your instrument you will play your best, even if you feel like you don't sound better than the last time you picked up your instrument.

CHAPTER 9: WHAT DO THE EXPERTS DO DIFFERENTLY?

"I've failed over and over and over again in my life and that is why I succeed."

-Michael Jordan

What is it that separates you from the internationally renowned musicians? What do they do differently? How do they think differently? How often have we heard the phrase "practice smarter, not harder"? Is that the key?

EXPERTS ARE MADE, NOT BORN

Research on this topic has been very extensive in recent years and the findings keep coming back consistently and overwhelmingly the same. Experts are made, not born! This means you can be that expert. You can be the eternally renowned musician. You can make and create yourself into what you want to be. Have you ever noticed in school or in orchestra how only some students seem to move ahead faster? Are you one of those that aren't moving as fast as you want to be? I know that I felt I wasn't moving fast enough. If you're feeling like I was feeling, it is not because you are less talented, slow, or dumb, but rather because you are not doing what the experts do.

DELIBERATE PRACTICE

Deliberate practice is working on **one single skill** that requires no more than 1-5 sessions or days to master. If you are working on a skill that takes you longer than 1-5 days to improve or master it, then it is too complex. You need to break it down or simplify it. Repeat this way of practicing with new skills each time one is mastered. With this kind of practice, you will slowly get better and better at your craft each and every day. It is important to realize that the importance of this kind of practice is not on quantity but on quality. Be aware though that both quality and quantity are necessary.

GOAL-ORIENTED PRACTICE

Having goal-oriented practice sessions means to have a specific result that you want to achieve. Be very clear in your mind about what you want to accomplish and do not stop working on it until you achieve it. Never simply put in your practice time without any goal or purpose. Doing this will only develop your skills of showing up to the practice room. Instead, be conscious of the skill you want to develop and don't stop working at it until the skill is developed.

FUNDAMENTALS

Fundamentals of your instrument are what you want to keep learning and improving constantly. Details in music account for only 10% of the final product; the fundamentals are what counts. Fundamentals include: scales, arpeggios, rhythm, pulse, intonation, tone colour, ear training, theory, hand placement and fingerings, breathing (for wind players), and the use of the bow (for string players). Experts are experts because they understand fundamentals better than anybody else and they are better at them than anybody else.

Consistently go back and practice the specific skill you need to master. Develop the habits and routines necessary to be always improving little by little every day.

MISTAKE AWARENESS

Be absolutely clear on why you made a mistake when you make them. Was it because of your fingers, hands, wrists, arms, air, bow...? Know specifically, down to the note, where the mistake happened. This kind of awareness will shine light on specific skills that you need to work on and improve. Professionals always see mistakes and so called "failures" as opportunities to learn, grow, and improve. Adopt this mentality into your own practice.

THREE QUESTIONS

The following are questions you should always be asking yourself:

1. What fundamental can I improve on?

Professionals are always improving on fundamentals.

2. Am I working on the next step?

Identify the steps you need to take and take action!

3. What am I missing?

One of the greatest pitfalls that almost everybody falls into is thinking that being a professional is a finish line. Being a professional is a journey. You must always and constantly improve yourself, grow, and learn; there is no end to that.

MOTIVATION

Following all of these steps requires lots of self-motivation and determination. These must be intrinsic, meaning coming from within. Do not ever make the mistake of chasing a dream or goal because of an exterior motive. It will let you down. An intrinsic one, however, is like a fire burning from within: you get to feed it all the wood you want. This will be the fuel that drives you forward.

PERSEVERANCE

Never giving up, never quitting, and always moving forward: these are the traits of experts. To become an expert, you must always persevere especially through tough challenges, because those experiences define you. It makes you stronger and allows you to grow, surpassing all those who would quit having to go through whatever you are going through. Watch motivational videos, listen to motivational speakers, and write down on paper that you will always persevere. Choose to commit yourself to continuous perseverance; it is the mark of an expert.

CHAPTER 10: MORE PRACTICE TIPS, TRICKS, THOUGHTS, AND IDEAS

"If I don't practice one day, I know it; two days, the critics know it; three days, the public knows it."

-Jascha Heifetz

Throughout this book, I have shown various ways of practicing. In this chapter, I want to show you 17 additional tips, tricks, thoughts, and ideas to add to your practice sessions. These are in no particular order.

TIP #1: PERFECT PRACTICE

We have all heard the saying "Practice makes perfect." Some people have gone one step further and said that "Perfect practice makes perfect." This may be true, but be aware that practice also makes permanent. Be very mindful of what you practice and how you practice, as mindless practice can be worse than not practicing at all.

TIP #2: PICK UP YOUR INSTRUMENT!

The hardest part of any journey is taking the first step. Open up your case, pick up your instrument and just start practicing. 90% of all success is simply showing up.

TIP #3: CHUNK YOUR PRACTICE

Split your practice into chunks, in as little as 10-20 minutes if needed, making your practice session easier and organized. This will help you avoid the unappealing thought of having to practice for hours on end. The ease of mind in knowing you don't have to practice for multiple hours will also help you take that first step to begin to practice.

TIP #4: YOU ARE YOUR GREATEST COMPETITION

Do not ever make the mistake of competing or comparing yourself with others! You are your greatest competition. Do not be bothered by other people's improvements or accomplishments. You may be proud of the happy with them, motivated by them, and desire to sound like them, but not let yourself be discouraged or distracted because of them. Focus on your own playing; always seek to better yourself.

TIP #5: STRETCH

Stretch before and after playing. Stretch your arms, hands, legs, and body. This will not only help prevent injuries, but will also wake up your body and get blood pumping to where it needs to go to play your instrument.

TIP #6: EXERCISE

Exercise is a vital part of a musician's wellbeing that is often overlooked. Remaining healthy and fit is crucial for endurance playing and for the longevity of your overall career. For all wind instrumentalists especially, a regular exercise routine will greatly aid in the development of lung capacity, air production, and air flow. A few hours a week running, swimming, or playing sports can transform your ability to play your instrument.

TIP #7: WRITE ON YOUR MUSIC

Make notes or observations for yourself on the music in the margins, under or over the notes. Mark down things to keep in mind such as phrasing, expression markings, and dynamic markings. Mark the beats and subdivisions for clear understanding of the rhythms. Mark the phrases and measures together to have a clear understanding of their direction. Chunk the music and break it down to make sense of it in your mind. Keep all the markings as clear and legible as possible.

TIP #8: WORK IN AND OUT OF PROBLEM SPOTS

When you are practicing challenging passages, ensure that you are also practicing going into the passage and coming out of it. Practice a few measures before the trouble area, and a few measures after. Train your brain to be confident with the passage in its approach, duration, and leaving the passage so that you do not panic during a performance when you are approaching the challenging area, or get distracted by your success when you finish the passage.

TIP #9: IF YOU CAN HEAR IT, YOU CAN PLAY IT

Hearing what you want to sound like is crucial to sounding like what you want to hear. You cannot sound like your favourite artist if you cannot hear that sound in your mind. Develop your mind's ear by listening to many recordings and familiarizing yourself with the aural definition of a beautiful tone on your instrument. Also practice singing your music to develop it in your mind. You can buzz your music as well if you are brass player. Improve the sound in your mind and the improvement of the physical sound of your instrument is sure to follow.

TIP #10: RECORD YOURSELF

Be sure to record yourself **at least** once a week. You don't need a high-tech recording device; just use your iPod, iPad, phone, or your computer. Track your progress when listening to your recordings. Know what you sound like and what you want to sound like. While listening, you can also identify trouble spots of which perhaps you were not aware. Turn on the metronome against your recording and see how well you play in time. Listen also to your intonation. Compare your recordings against professional recordings that you may want to sound like.

TIP #11: ASSOCIATE COLOURS

This tip works well for some, but not for others. Try to associate and visualize colours to different sounds that you play. Hear the sound and try to see the colour that it depicts. You can use this to help you develop your tone or as mentioned before, to memorize music.

TIP #12: TRACE YOUR NOTES

Trace and connect all the notes with a line. Draw a line that follows the placement of the notes on the page and notice the patterns it makes. This will help you get a sense of the phrase, direction, and climax of the music.

TIP #13: VARIED RHYTHMS

Varied rhythms are useful for fast runs and passages. Diversifying the rhythms will help you keep your practicing engaged and focused while also enabling you to play evenly. There are many ways to vary rhythms. You can play dotted rhythms such as in Figure 1. You can also experiment playing the run in groups of three notes such as in Figure 2. For more diversification, play the run in groups of four notes, five notes, as well as in triplets as shown in Figure 3. Come up with new ways of varying the rhythms for your fast passages. Note that when you play a varied rhythm, you should also play the opposite varied rhythm immediately after. See A vs. B in the figures below.

Figure 1

Figure 2

Figure 3

C

TIP #14: THE FIVE WHYS

Use the five whys technique whenever you run into any sort of problem or mistake to analyze how to improve. When you encounter a problem, ask yourself "why", answer the question, ask "why" to that answer, and so on. For example, I missed a high D:

Why? Because I got really tense.

Why? I was scared.

Why? I have never played for a large group before.

In this case it only took three whys to get a better understanding of why that high D was missed. You could keep asking why to find deeper roots to problems. This strategy helps to isolate issues and come up with solutions.

TIP #15: START IN DIFFERENT PLACES

Vary your practice sessions by starting in different sections in your music. You can learn a piece from the end to the beginning instead of the beginning to the end, or start in the middle. Practicing this way enables you to start playing from any measure anywhere in the music, which also aids in memorizing.

TIP #16: IMMEDIATE VIRTUOSITY

Practice picking up your instrument and playing a virtuosic passage or piece as the first notes of the day. Warm-ups or note checks are unnecessary – play with confidence. Have the first notes that come out of your instrument be a challenging virtuosic section. This will give you a clear sense of where you are in terms of skill and development of the piece, and even in range expansion. This kind of practice sets you up for those emergency situations when you need to pick up your instrument cold out of its case and just play.

TIP # 17: COACHING

Find a friend or family member that can meet with you once every week or two to keep you accountable and encourage you to expand yourself and grow. If you can afford it, you can hire a professional coach. Set goals together, develop your career plan and your desired outcome for the coming weeks. When you meet up you can discuss your strengths, weaknesses, struggles, successes, failures, and opportunities. This is a time for self-analysis and self-development.

CHAPTER 11: THINGS TO KEEP IN MIND

"Perseverance is the hard work you do after you get tired of doing the hard work you already did."

-Newt Gingrich

As this book comes to a close, I want to quickly go over some of what we have learned and also give you some ideas to keep in mind.

Always remember that your **goals** are the most important. It is the first step to turning any dream or thought into reality. Without goals, you are inevitably going nowhere. Have goals and make them real by writing them down.

Simplicity is your friend. Focus on only one thing at a time, whether that is your breathing, bow movement, notes, sound, or fingers. Always ask yourself the **golden question**: If I could master one skill today, which skill would make the biggest difference in my playing? Ask a variation of this question after you have done a run-through of your piece or if you are short on time, such as: If I could master one section today, which would make the biggest difference in my playing?

Chunk your music to simplify it. Break it down by phrases and sub-phrases. Do whatever you need to do to keep it simple!

Don't waste your time playing passages you already know well and can play. Focus on the practicing what you can't play. That is where improvement lies.

Always do, don't try. Remember that trying only gives you the permission to fail and give up. When you decide to "do", keep in mind that you will have setbacks and mistakes, but also remember that those setbacks and mistakes are opportunities to grow. They are opportunities to learn and are a step in the right direction. Simply "do" or "don't do".

As you are trying new strategies and techniques, remember to **do what works** for you and stop doing what doesn't work. You can always come back to them later. People's practicing strategies and techniques continuously change throughout the years. Keep this book close by and revisit some of the tips that perhaps you were not yet ready to add to your practicing at a different point in your life.

Finally, this saying holds true for all areas of life and should be taken to heart: **Patience and perseverance always wins**. This is what separates the professionals from non-professionals. Commit yourself to saying this every day until it becomes habit and gets cemented in your subconscious. Be patient and persevere and you will attain your goals. That is my hope for you and I know you will succeed in whatever you undertake.

CONCLUSION

Thank you once again for downloading this book! I really hope this book was a great help in your approach to practicing and I hope that over time you will continuously see and hear the benefits you have gained from this book.

Don't stop at just reading this book. Pick and choose one strategy that you learned that you can apply to your practicing today.

Finally, if you have enjoyed this book and received any value from it, I ask if you would be so kind to take a few short moments to leave a review on Amazon. It would be an encouragement to me and helpful to anybody looking to improve their playing.

Search "Music Practice" on Amazon to find this book and leave a review.

Thank you and all the best in your practicing!

MOTIVATIONAL VIDEOS

Please note that these links may not work as the videos may be removed at the time of reading this book.

How bad do you want it? What are you willing to do and give up to achieve success?:

https://www.youtube.com/watch?v=lsSC2vx7zFQ

A powerful video: you can do whatever you decide to do in your life:

https://www.youtube.com/watch?v=xeBHshlQu88

A great video about never giving up and pushing forward:

https://www.youtube.com/watch?v=AFGWnqNf6t0

Inspirational video with quotes and messages from various successful people:

https://www.youtube.com/watch?v=2TBQX-FJjfk

A great compilation of various motivational materials, this video is great to listen to while going for a walk, run, or just to have in the background:

https://www.youtube.com/watch?v=ZmAFMNmSKus

Words of wisdom and motivation by Michael Jordan:

https://www.youtube.com/watch?v=gfvuF5qf9v0

Steve Job's motivational commencement speech at Stanford University:

https://www.youtube.com/watch?v=UF8uR6Z6KLc

Secrets to success by Will Smith:

https://www.youtube.com/watch?v=q5nVqeVhgQE

Various keys to success and motivation by Tony Robbins:

https://www.youtube.com/watch?v=hR51VfCeWSA

An eye opener for success and productivity by Brian Tracy:

https://www.youtube.com/watch?v=6Pz03hNEVTE

Secrets of self-made millionaires talk by Brian Tracy. Tips, advice, and ideas used by successful millionaires in our society:

https://www.youtube.com/watch?v=gUWOl7jcQro

MASTERCLASSES

Please note that these links may not work as the videos may be removed at the time of reading this book.

Itzhak Perlman Masterclass Q&A:

https://www.youtube.com/watch?v=OFu7BGIO3s4

Joyce DiDonato Voice Masterclasses:

https://www.youtube.com/watch?v=o3QAvSAoA_8

https://www.youtube.com/watch?v=unIaEe0Nw88

https://www.youtube.com/watch?v=9dNQhI3S5_w

Daniel Barenboim Piano Masterclass:

https://www.youtube.com/watch?v=14dwegqniNg

Maxim Vengerov Violin Masterclass:

https://www.youtube.com/watch?v=Wpp7oxrBUq0

Emmanuel Pahud Flute Masterclass:

https://www.youtube.com/watch?v=Cm7UfC8swis

Yo-Yo Ma Cello and Orchestra Masterclass:

https://www.youtube.com/watch?v=MPqCi9ywzOc

Berlin Philharmonic Winds Masterclass Q&A:

https://www.youtube.com/watch?v=SdAnogOKR0I

https://www.youtube.com/watch?v=yUxY7tagf0g

https://www.youtube.com/watch?v=oKIIDJOt7DA

https://www.youtube.com/watch?v=_21jqCDiPFE

https://www.youtube.com/watch?v=jIVl9ubQR_o

CONNECT WITH DAVID

Thank you so much for taking the time to read this book. I'm really excited for you to start on the path to success in your practicing.

If you have any questions, concerns, or comments, please feel free to contact me directly at: dave.a.dumais@gmail.com

We have a Facebook group for readers just like you who want to take their music performance to the next level. In this group we will be sharing tips and strategies for practice, performance, and success. This is also a great way to make connections and have your questions answered. Come join us on Facebook: http://on.fb.me/1HrTW65

You can also follow me on Twitter: @davida_dumais

All the best to you!

David Dumais

ABOUT THE AUTHOR

David Dumais is a musician, performer, teacher, and author who always seeks to better himself and help others do the same. He currently resides in Ottawa, Canada. David loves to educate and inspire others to achieve success and live their dreams.

Learn more at: http://amzn.to/1Co8gQX

:

Made in the USA
San Bernardino, CA
03 November 2019